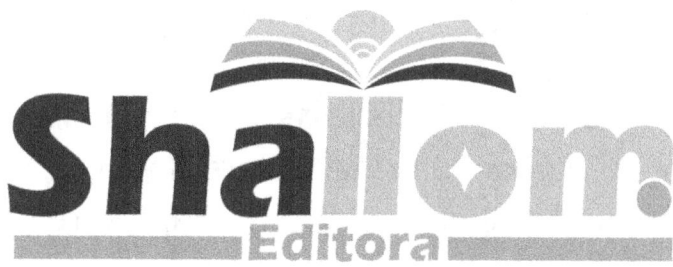

Hello little artists! Welcome to an exciting and colorful journey through our children's coloring book. Get ready to explore a universe full of fun, imagination and endless creative possibilities!

In this enchanted book, you will find a collection of captivating drawings, ready to be filled with the most vibrant and vivid colors your imaginations can create. From adorable animals to stunning landscapes and fantastical characters, every page is full of adventures waiting to be explored.

Coloring is more than just an activity; It's an opportunity to express your creativity, experiment with colors and immerse yourself in a world of fantasy. So, grab your colored pencils, crayons and markers, and embark on this exciting journey with us!

We look forward to seeing your unique and wonderful creations. So, get ready to dive into the pages of this book and let your imagination fly!

Have fun coloring!

**AUTHOR OF THE BOOK:** ARLINDO ARTUR MARQUES
**ILLUSTRATIONS**: HDprimos Marques
**PUBLISHER:** SHALLOM EDITORA

**CONTACTO:** +258 84 784 7663    **E-MAIL:** arlindoarturmarques30@gmail.com

# INSTRUCTIONS FOR USE

**1. Choose your Coloring Materials:** Before you start, choose the materials you like to use for coloring. Colored pencils, crayons, markers and even watercolors are great options. Make sure you have a flat, protected surface to work on.

**2. Explore the Pages:** Take a look at all the pages in the book and choose the ones that catch your attention the most. You can start from the first page or skip to whichever drawing you want to color first.

**3. Be Creative:** Don't be afraid to be creative! Use a variety of colors and try different combinations to make the designs even more interesting. There are no rules, just have fun!

**4. Take Care of Your Tools:** Remember to take care of your coloring supplies to make them last longer. Keep your colored pencils sharp, close marker caps when not in use, and clean crayons after each coloring session.

**5. Share Your Art:** Once you've finished coloring a page, feel free to share your masterpiece with friends and family. You can also frame it and display it proudly on your wall!

**6. Explore Your Creativity:** In addition to coloring within the lines, feel free to add your own personal touches to the drawings. You can draw extra backgrounds, add stickers, or even create your own stories based on the characters.

**7. Have fun:** The most important thing is to have fun! Coloring is a relaxing and therapeutic activity, so enjoy every moment and let your imagination run wild.

## PERSONAL INFORMATION

FULL NAME....................................................... ...................................
DATE OF BIRTH..............................................................................
MY FAVORITE DRAWING ................................................... ..............

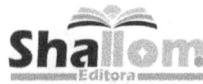

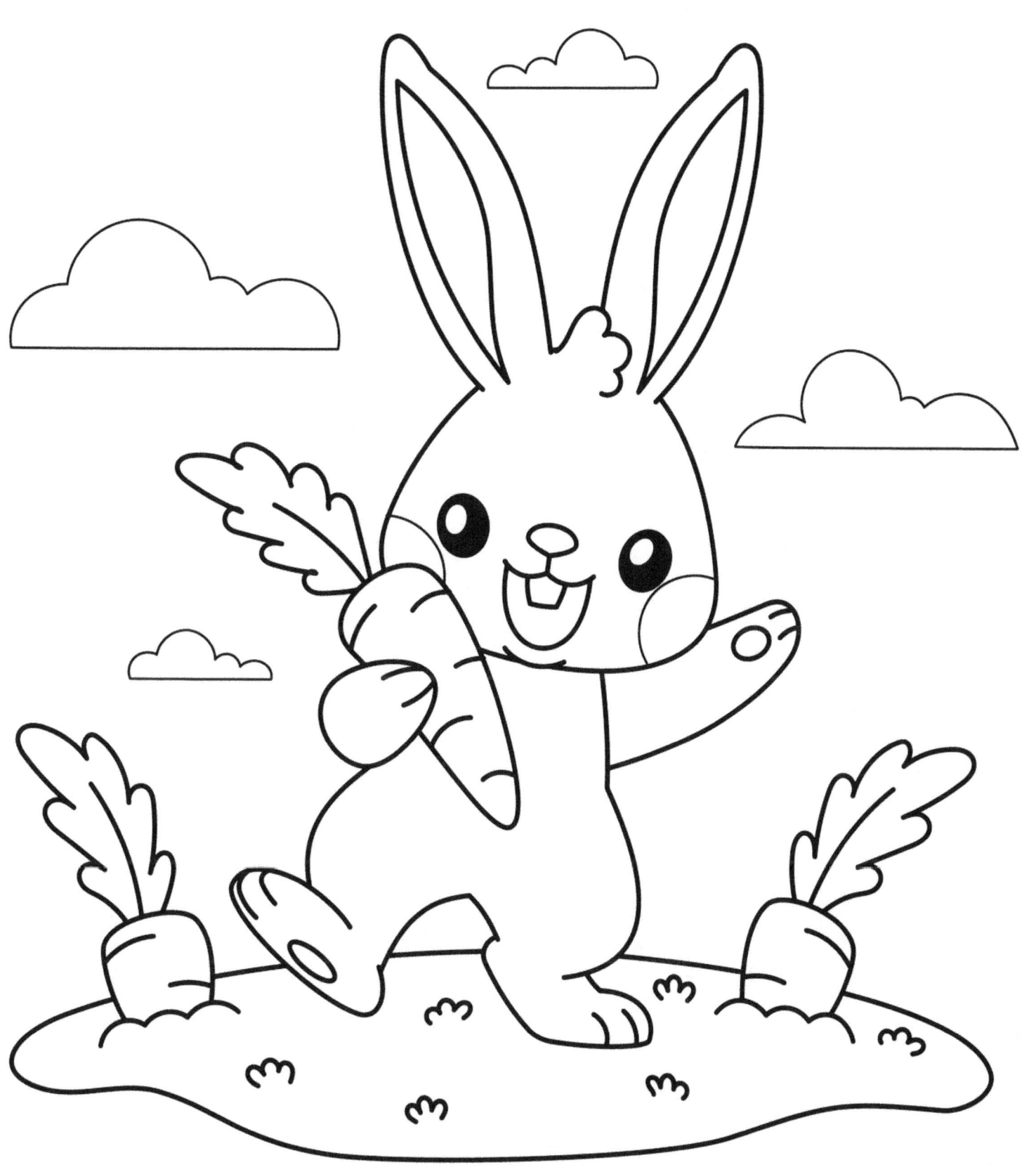

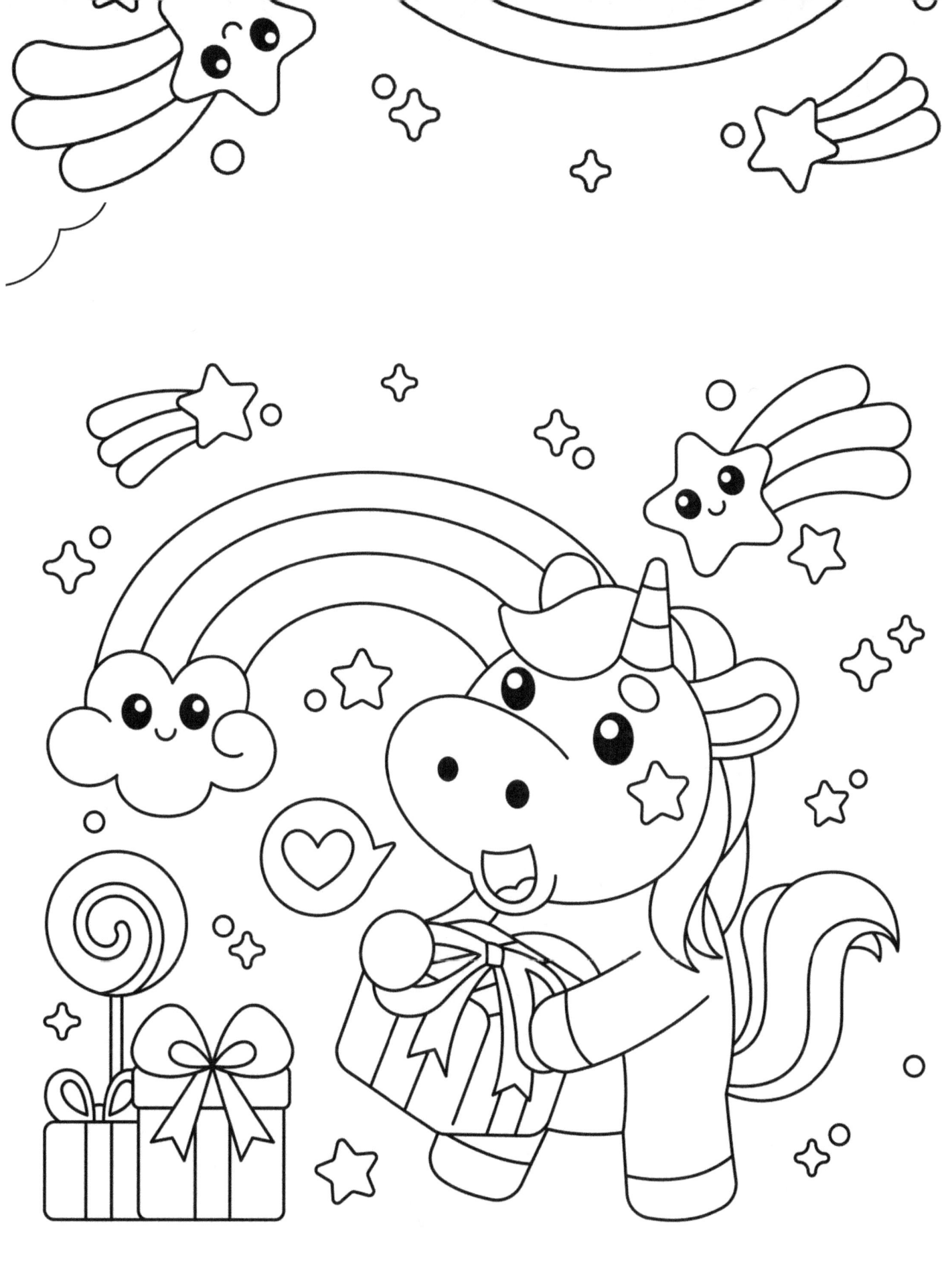

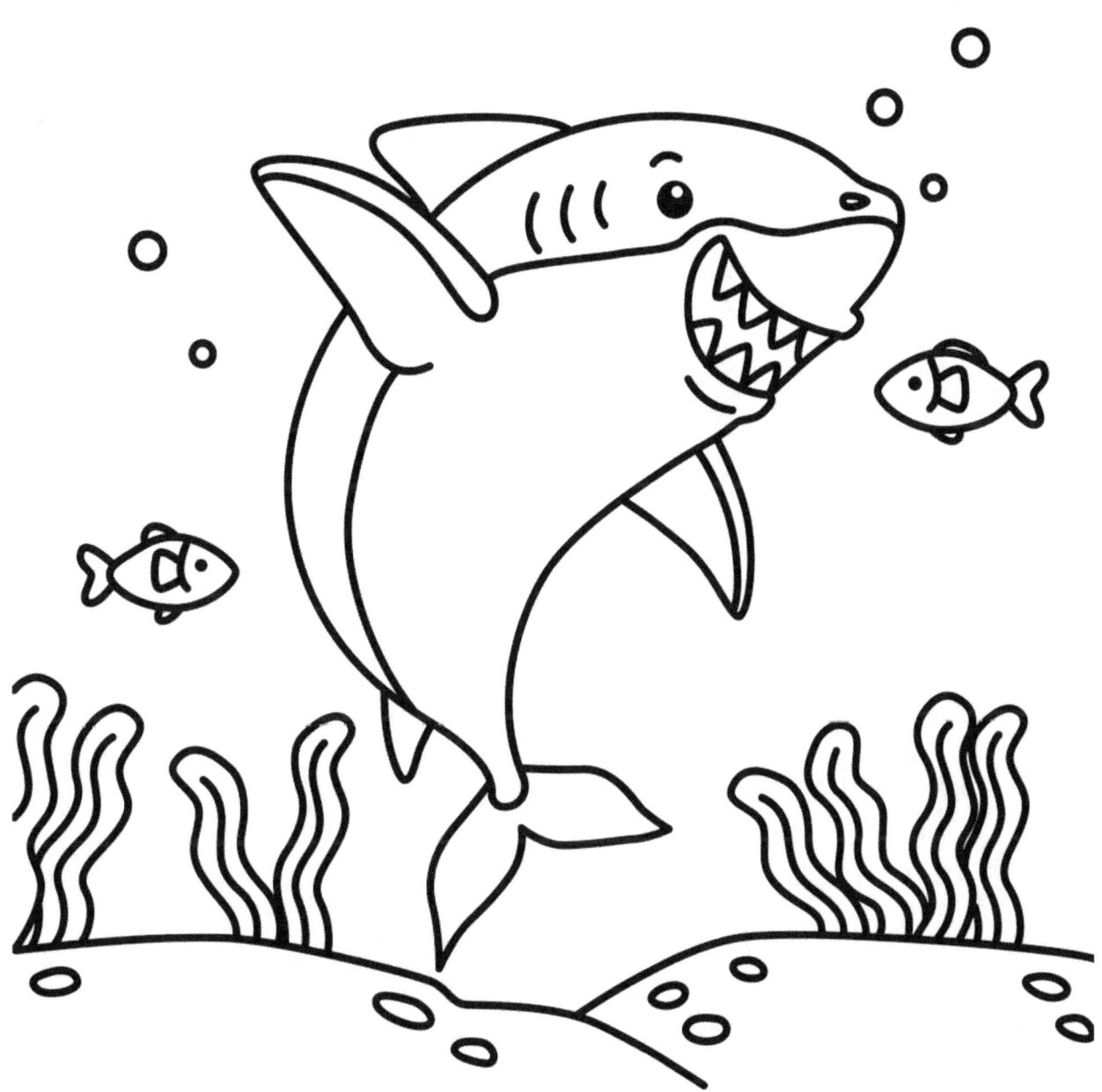

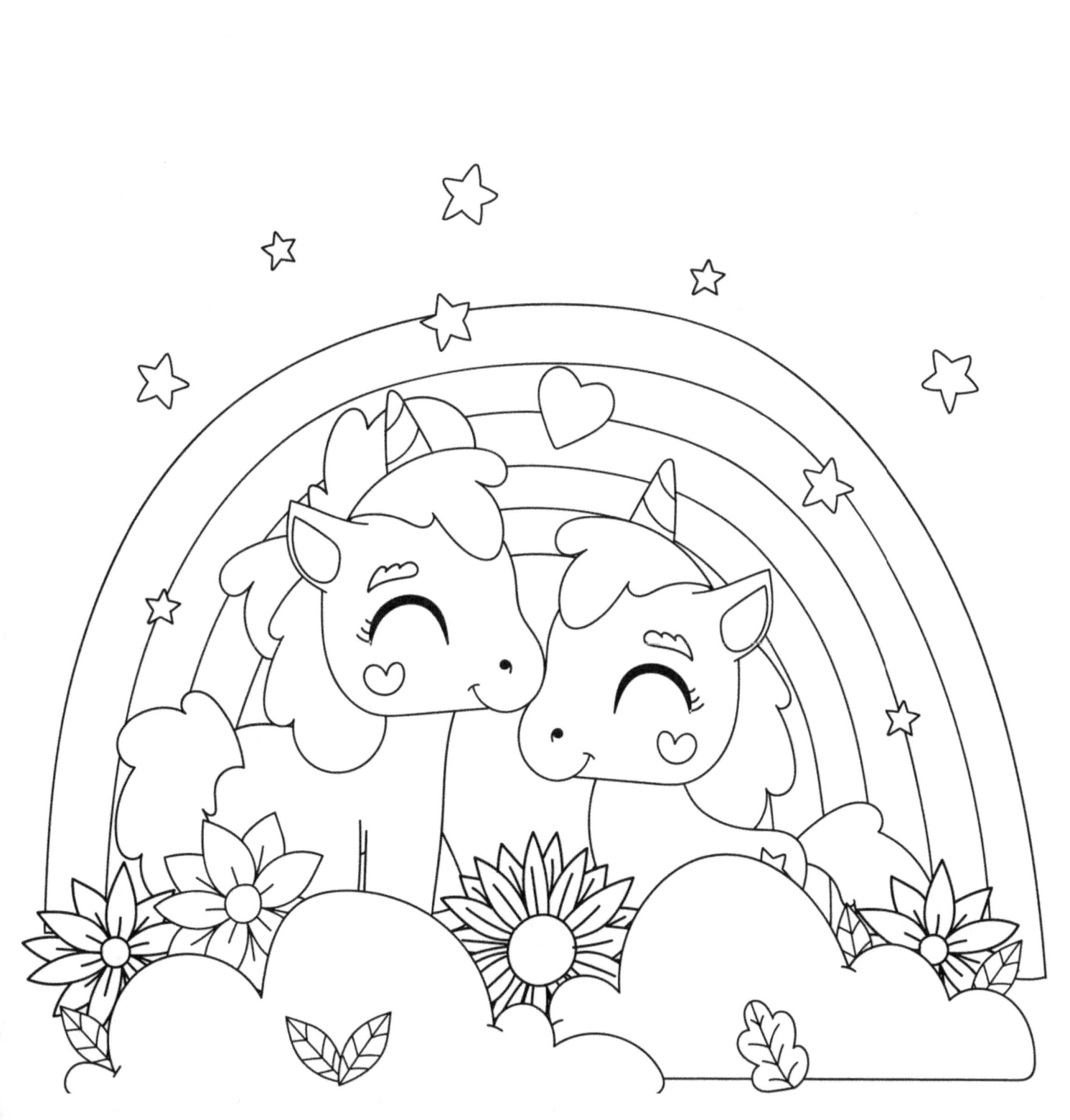

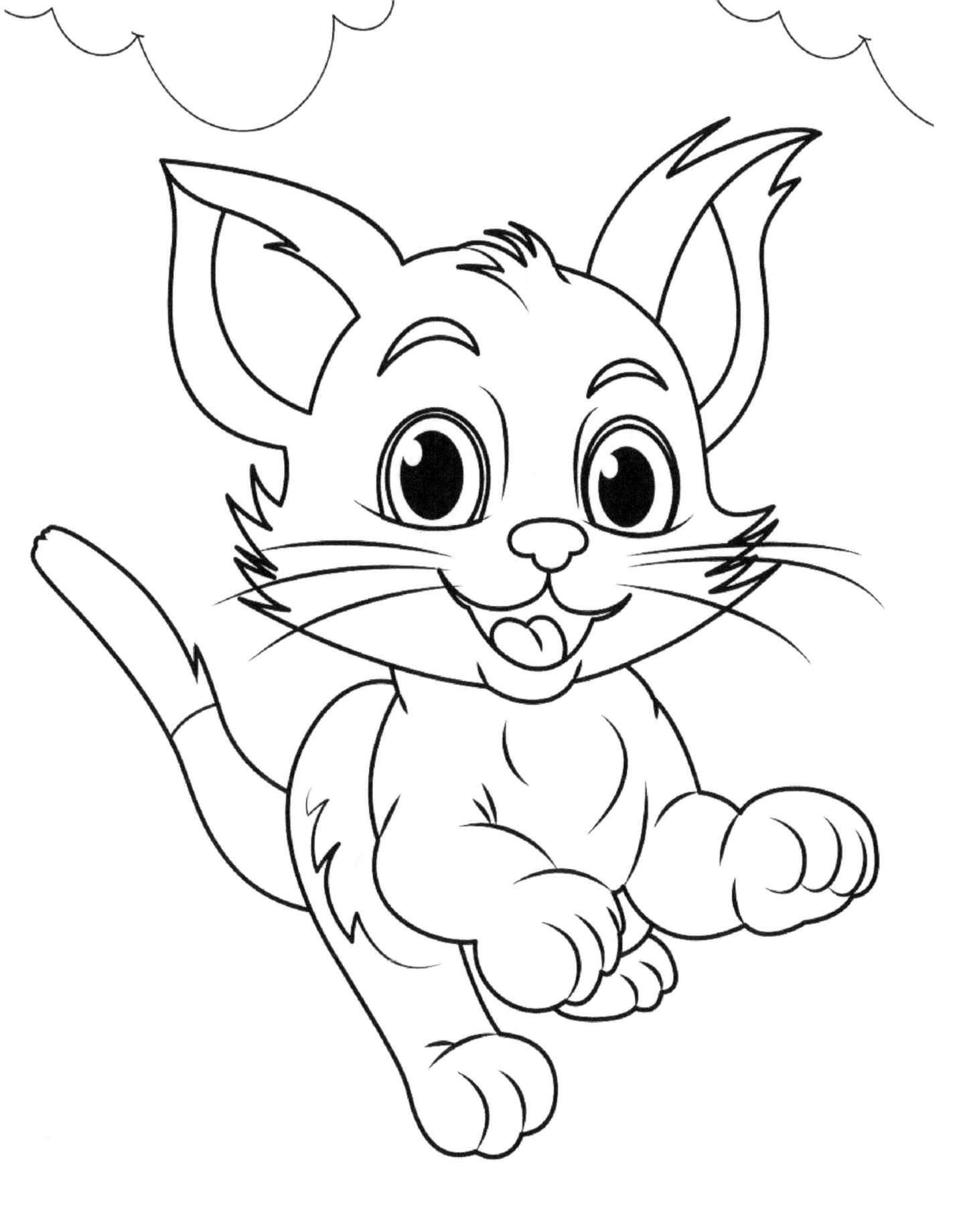

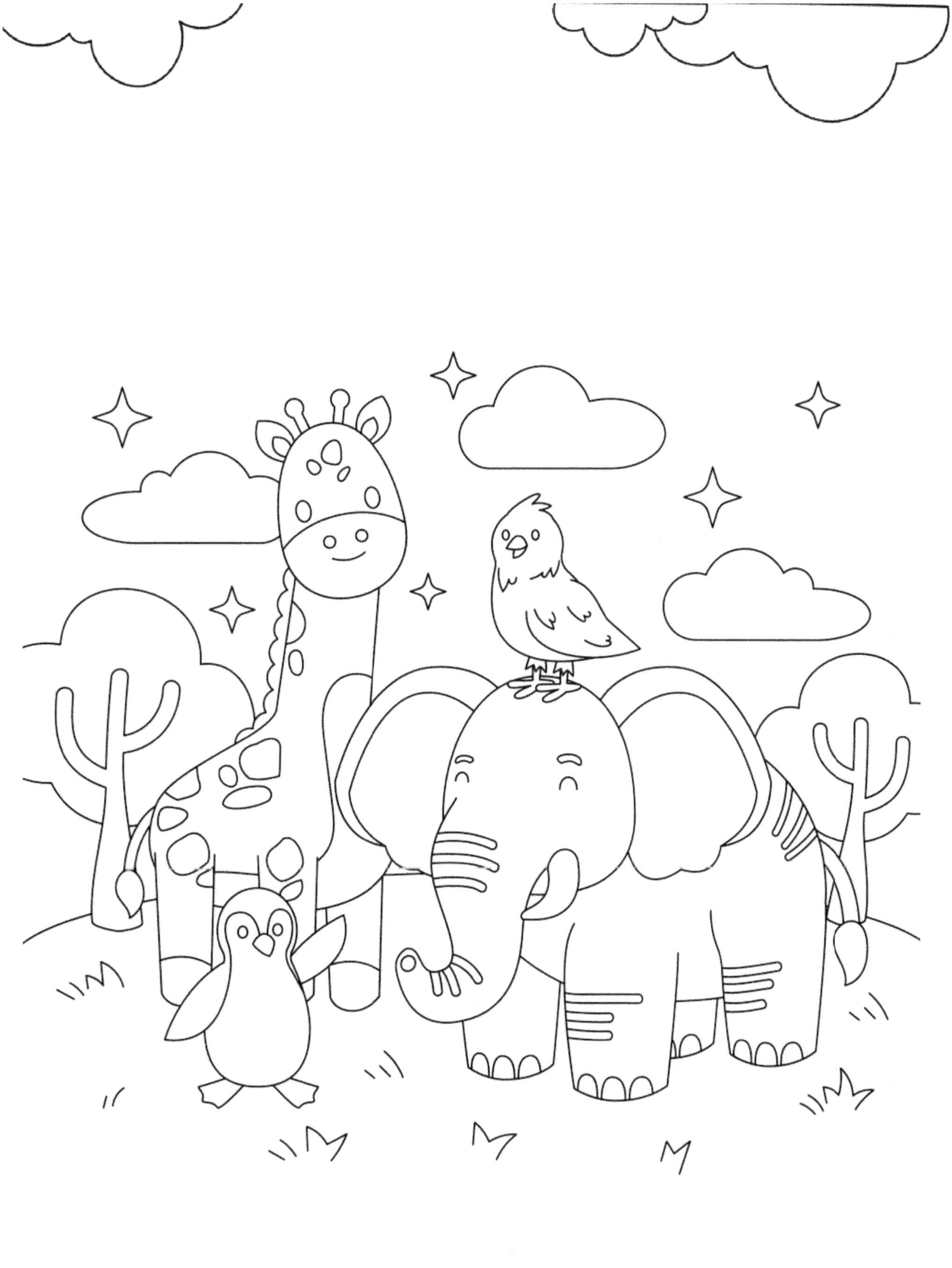

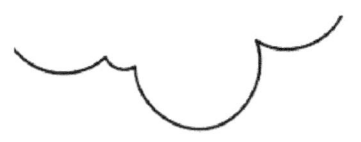
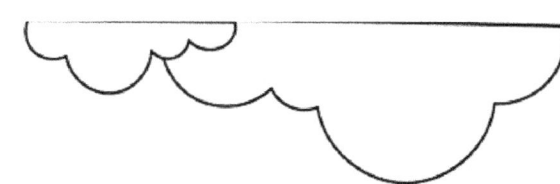

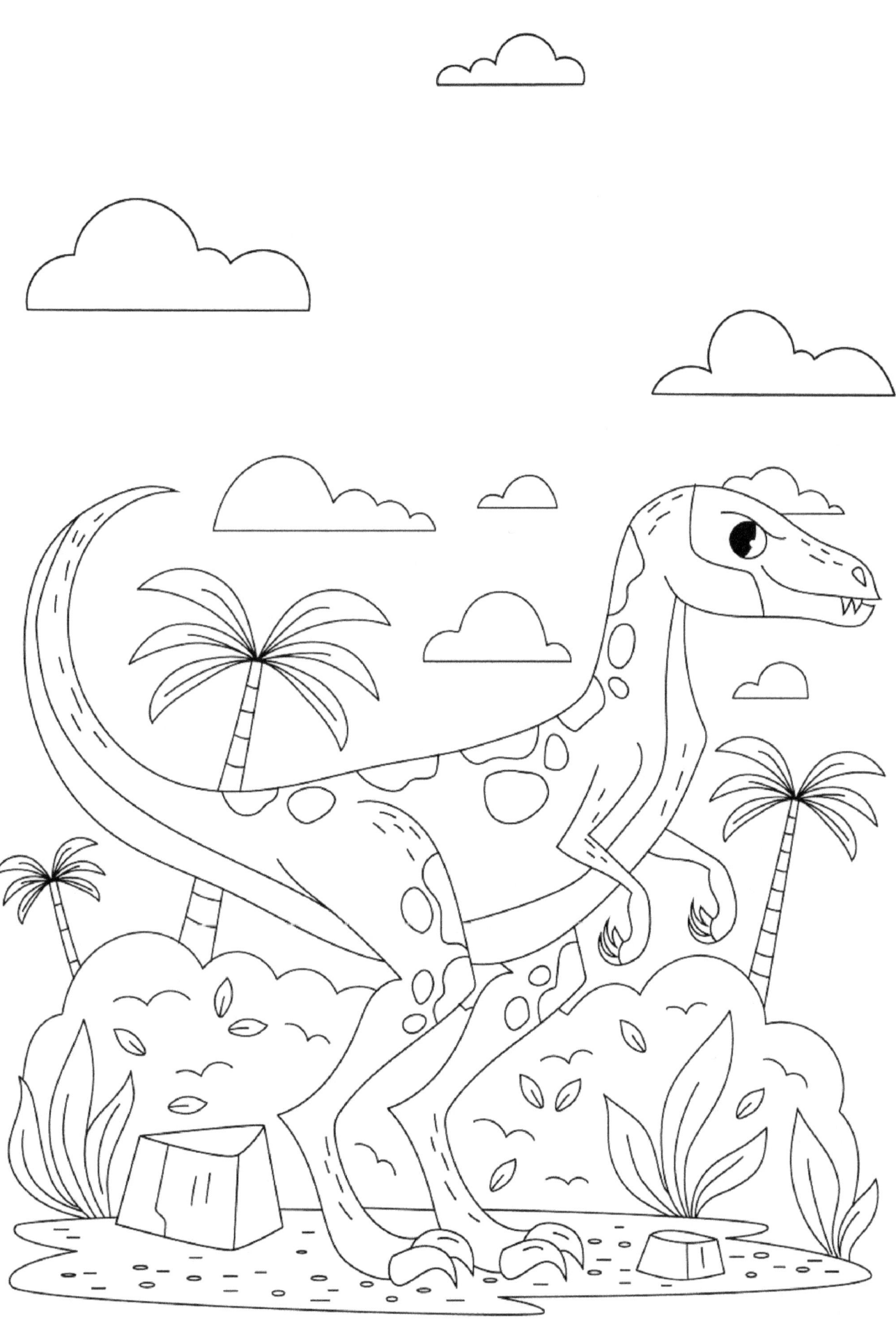

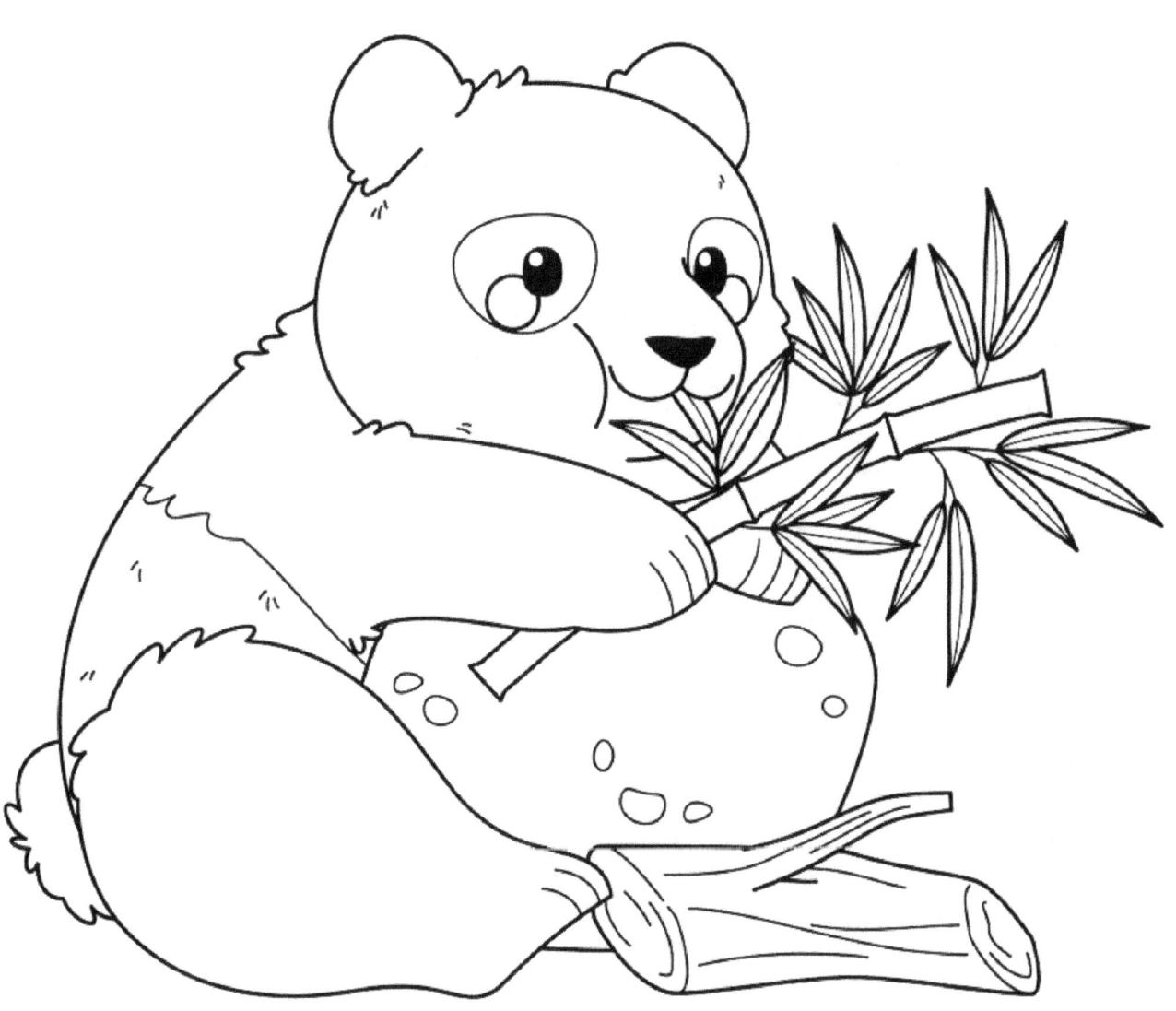

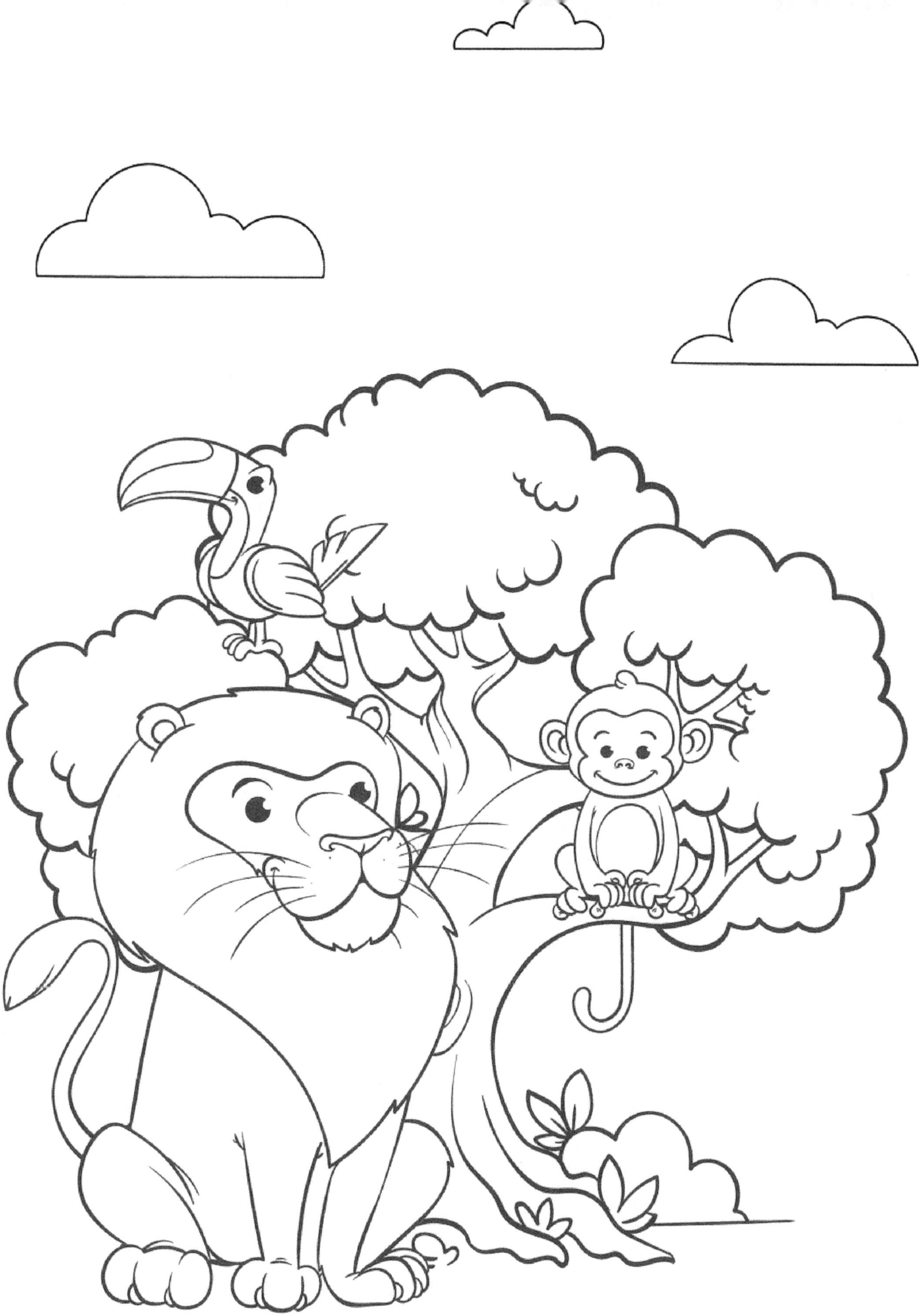

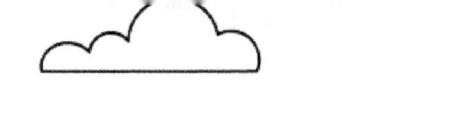

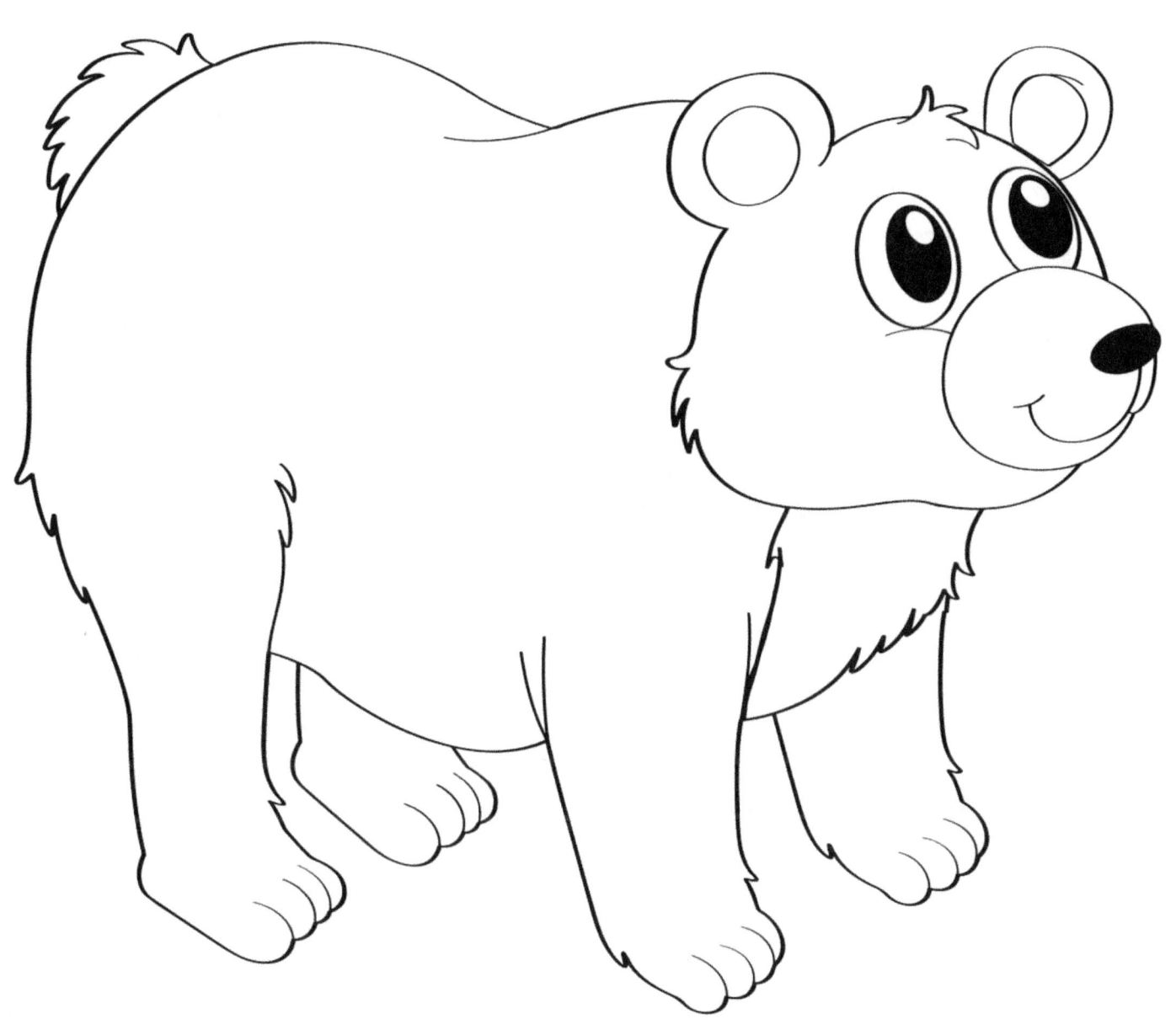

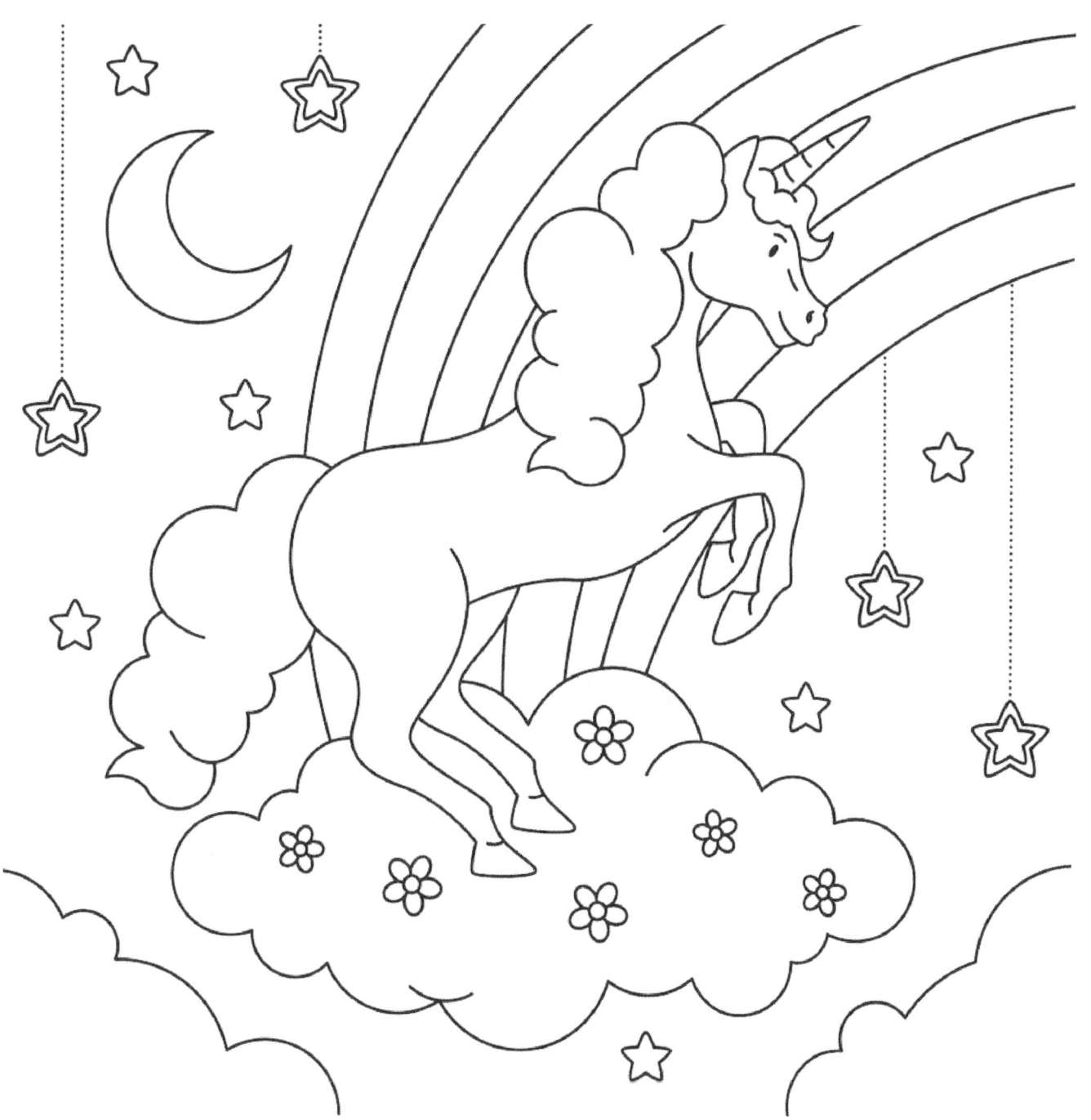

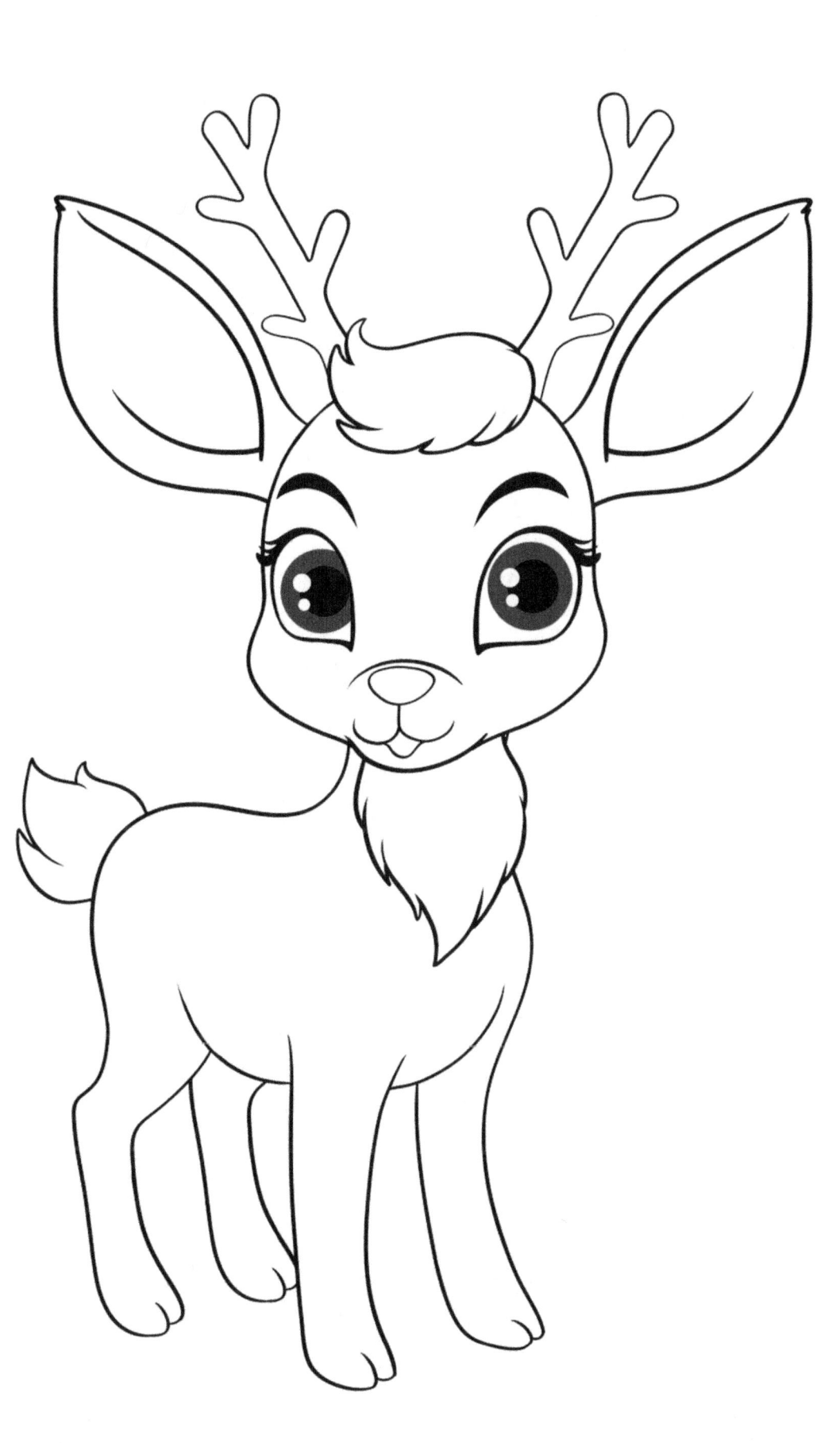

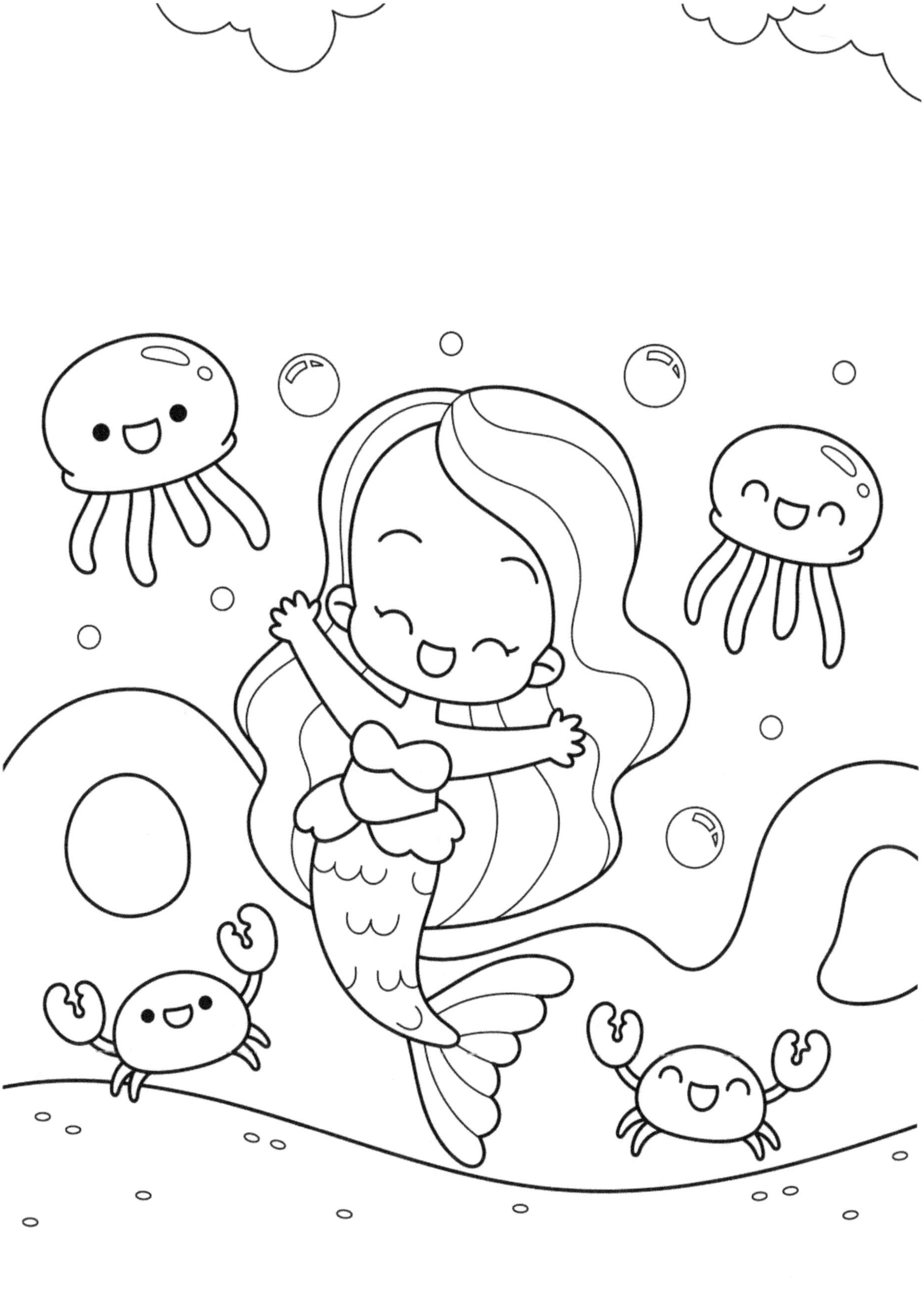

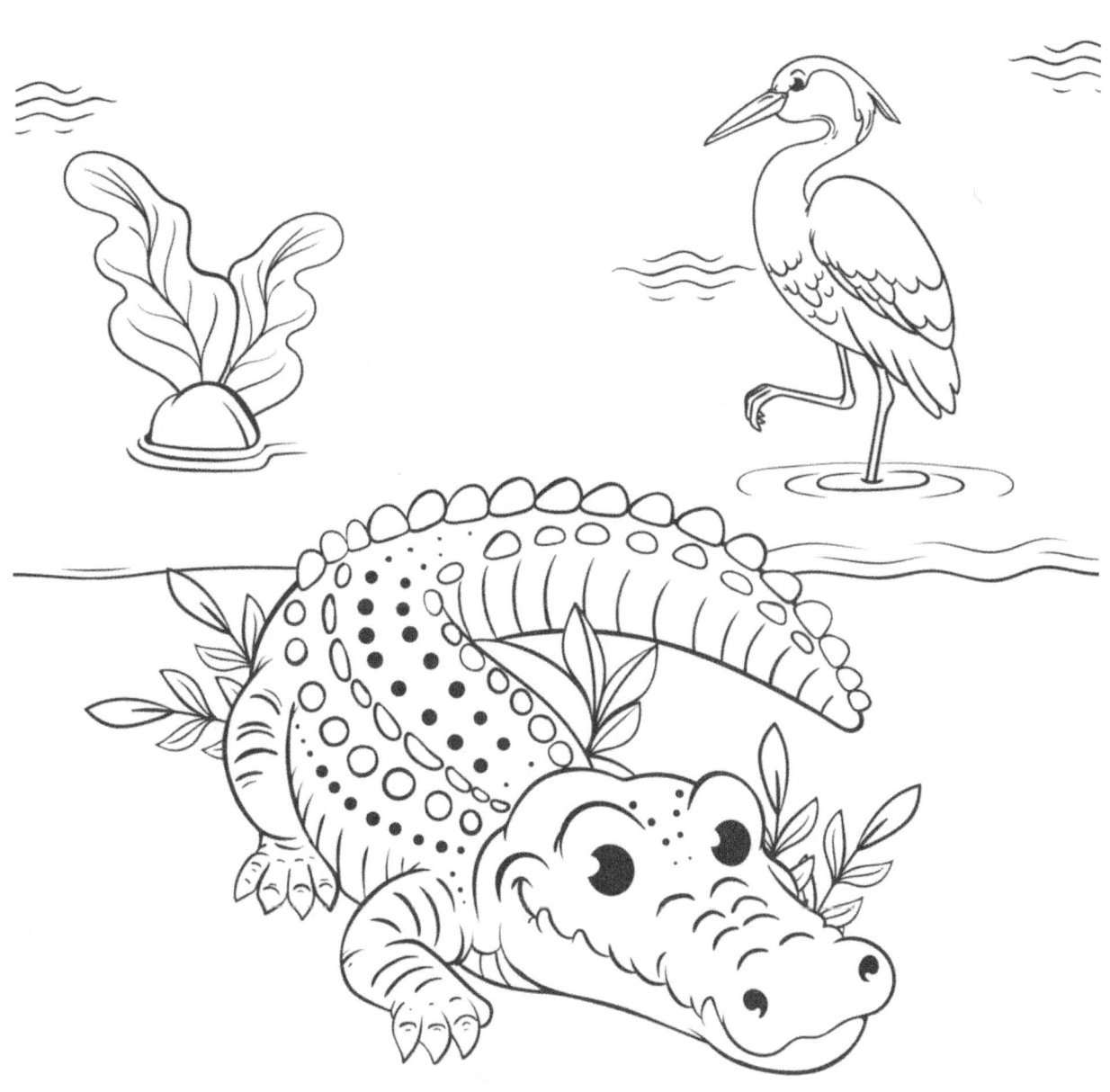

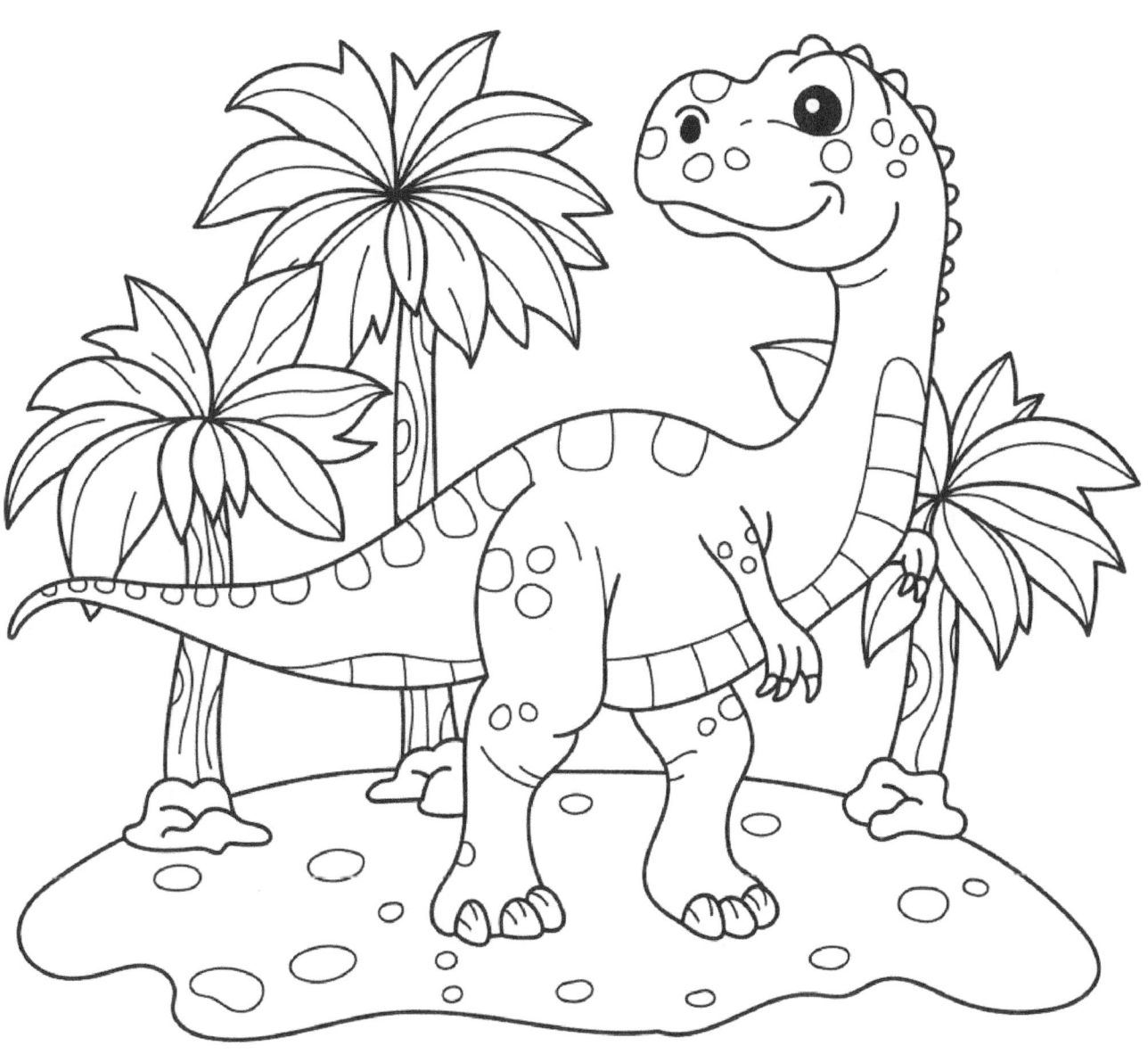

www.ingramcontent.com/pod-product-compliance
Lightning Source LLC
Chambersburg PA
CBHW062237220526
45471CB00009B/3513